Boldly ENCOURAGED

A PERSONAL JOURNEY OF FAITH AND HOPE

Encouraging devotionals for our daily lives

Sandra A. McManus

ISBN 979-8-89043-898-0 (paperback)
ISBN 979-8-89043-899-7 (hardcover)
ISBN 979-8-89043-900-0 (digital)

Copyright © 2023 by Sandra A. McManus

All rights reserved. No part of this publication may be reproduced, distributed, or transmitted in any form or by any means, including photocopying, recording, or other electronic or mechanical methods without the prior written permission of the publisher. For permission requests, solicit the publisher via the address below.

Christian Faith Publishing
832 Park Avenue
Meadville, PA 16335
www.christianfaithpublishing.com

Printed in the United States of America

This book is dedicated to my loving husband and best friend, Jeff, and our sons, Andrew and William.

Contents

Preface vii

What His Hands Do 1
Once Lost and Now Found 3
Do All to the Glory of God 5
Rely on Your Equipment 7
Have a Mentor 10
Refine Your Thinking 12
Happy Christmas 14
Quiet Time 16
Happy New Year 18
How Is Your Compassion 20
The Good Shepherd 22
When We Don't Obey 24
Thanking God for Prayers That Took Years 26
The 21-Day Fix 30
The Cure 32
The Thankfulness Jar 34
We All Need a Coach 36
My Worth Is Not in What I Own 38
Alienation 40
How to Survive a Rough Day 42
The Enemy 44
Divine Appointment 46
Betrayal 49

He Sets You High on a Rock 51
God Is a God of Order 53
Hummingbirds...55
Do Demons Really Exist? 57
When Someone Holds You Up in Prayer 59
The Walls of Blackness Castle 61

Epilogue 65
One Day I Dreamed 67
The Romans Road 70
The Attributes of God 71
The Sinner's Prayer 72
Key Bible Verses for Special Situations 73

Preface

IN 2014, I WAS challenged by a faithful church member to pick ten Facebook friends, create a group, and then let them know that I would pray for them. In turn, each person from that group would be asked to do the same. This was to be an exercise using the concept of multiplicity, and the goal was to multiply encouragement to as many people in the Antelope Valley in Lancaster and Palmdale, California, as possible. In taking this challenge, and to be a true blessing to my selected group of ladies, I wanted to include some words of encouragement to let them know that I really did care and would certainly pray for them. Through much prayer, I was able to write numerous devotionals and words of encouragement. I had no idea that this idea would turn into an inspiration from the Holy Spirit to write about my everyday life and real-world challenges, as well as to convey ways to encourage each other in the context of my daily life experiences.

I have always enjoyed long walks, and I have found that these walks are a great time to think, pray, and organize the day. What transpired from this time was truly amazing to me, and I found that I would not only receive the ideas for my writing; but I would also receive some incredible, inspiring, and meaningful lessons as well. During my daily walks, I genuinely felt as if God was right there, next to me, telling me what these ladies needed to hear every week for encouragement! I would come home, write notes, expand on the ideas, and prayerfully write about it and post it. God never left me on my own for ideas and always showed up on my walks.

This book is a compilation of the "still small voice" that filled my heart and thoughts for over two years and provided me with many inspiring words that I posted for this group of ten women. I sincerely hope these short and simple posts will comfort, inspire, and encourage you as you navigate your way through this journey we call life. May God bless you and extend His grace to you and your families.

What His Hands Do

HAVE YOU EVER THOUGHT about everything your hands do? Every moment of every day, we are using our hands to perform some amazing things. Our hands have twenty-seven bones, and our fingers have thousands of very dense nerve endings. If you have ever had a paper cut, you know how much it hurts even though the cut is so small. Hands also have such incredible tactile and sensory feedback to our brains. Do you remember the first time your husband held your hand? Did you get a lightning bolt shooting up your arm with a sense of warmth and goodness like I did?

As a nurse, I've used my hands to start IVs, insert catheters, assess lungs, perform chest compressions, and comfort fearful and hurting patients and family members. We use our hands to cook meals, clean the house, plant flowers, feed our children, and clean up messes. Students use their hands to write papers, and teachers use their hands to correct them. Choir directors use their hands to direct singing voices in choirs, and music conductors use their hands to synchronize music with hundreds of musical instruments in orchestras. We use our hands for everything from the smallest touch in caring for a baby to rapid and complicated medical procedures, such as CPR and lifesaving operations.

I've been thinking a lot about God and how He uses His hands. Did you know that the word *hand* has over 1,400 references in the Bible? At this very moment, God has His hands open ready to rain down blessings, protection, and help if we just open our hands to receive it. Jesus used His hands to heal the sick, preach, eat, teach, and turn over the money changers' tables in the temple. Many people were literally touched by Jesus's hands. Those same hands would be nailed to a cross for our sins as Jesus paid the price for our eternal salvation. Someday we will feel the touch of His hands when we see Him face to face.

The hand of God can comfort you, guide you, lead you, and give you peace and joy. Right now, the hand of God is leading us through the strife of major social and political changes and will someday usher us into eternity with Him. Isn't it nice to know that there is a pair of warm, strong hands waiting for us to grasp and hold whenever we need them? Jesus said in John 10:28–29: "And I give unto them eternal life; and they shall never perish, neither shall any man pluck them out of my hand. My Father, which gave them me, is greater than all; and no man is able to pluck them out of my Father's hand." You can rest assured that you are safe and secure in His hands. May you know His comfort, reassurance, and His incredible love.

Once Lost and Now Found

THIS LAST MONTH, OUR family has been riddled with a plethora of difficulties and major challenges. A few of the highlights have been: food poisoning, bronchitis, a broken wrist, an asthma attack, a sinus infection, and even a lost set of keys. Without God in my life and the comfort of the Holy Spirit, I would not have survived this particular season of my life.

The sinus infection cleared, the broken wrist was set, the food poisoning resolved, and the respiratory issues improved. God took care of these problems; however, the lost set of keys remained unresolved.

I think the issue that bothered me the most was the lost set of keys. It was a complete set with keys for the house, the mailbox, and keys for two vehicles! I was so concerned that I reached out to a few friends to pray that they would be found as soon as possible. I continued to pray myself, but worry took over my thoughts and I began to have visions of thieves breaking into the house, stealing everything I had and putting my most cherished possessions in our cars as they drove away. I figured they would stop at the mailbox on their way out and steal our identity too! I realized that taking my eyes off of God just made the problem worse, and I had to give up complete control to Him and really believe that all would work out in His timing.

Once I did that, the most amazing thing happened. Several weeks passed, and upon returning home from the tutor, I saw the keys hanging on our front door knocker! No note, no explanation whatsoever. What a wonderful surprise and such a valuable lesson for me as I learned to pray and trust God! What a miracle. Who found them and put them there? We will never know, but He does.

Romans 14:17 says, "For the kingdom of God is not meat and drink, but righteousness, and peace, and joy in the Holy Spirit."

I am so thankful for the Holy Spirit who treats me as His treasure and possession. He is the helper that never leaves my side and gives me continued guidance and wisdom. Dependance on God works. Prayer works. God will make a way when all we see is an impossible and hopeless situation. Trusting Him completely is never easy, but it is always worth the effort. Know that you are loved and cared for by God. He is the friend that never leaves your side. He brings peace and joy even when trials come.

Do All to the Glory of God

HAVE YOU EVER WONDERED what it means to do all to the glory of God?

When I was in my twenties listening to sermons in church, I would get perplexed when the preacher encouraged us to do *all* to the glory of God. I couldn't understand how a holy and mighty God could care about me doing dishes or cleaning the toilet. After all, didn't He have better things to do, like stopping wars, curing disease, and protecting missionaries in New Guinea? Did God even have time to care about my measly and seemingly insignificant woes? I felt like God was the admiral of a large ship. He stayed at the bow high in the pilot tower. I stayed in the fourth-class deck in the back of the ship. I was far from Him. I was allowed to reach Him for catastrophic issues like major leaks in the hull, but the mundane things like a rat infestation or leaky toilet were up to me to fix. However, God began to convince me that He was more than capable of caring about both the big and small at the same time. My view of God was way off the mark, and I only called on Him for major emergencies. I always dealt with everything else on my own. Having that kind of relationship with God was so limiting. It caused me so much stress and anxiety. I realized that I was making everything so much harder on myself.

Because I lacked the truth and knowledge that God cares about every single detail of my personal life: I was not able to understand that I could receive peace, rest, comfort, and even the desires of my own heart. God knows our needs. We need to be willing to go to Him for even the most mundane activities in our day. I needed to learn about the attributes of God and put them at the forefront of my schedule. I began to focus on His sovereignty, His trustworthiness, His love, His patience, His power, His grace, and His glory. I began to focus on the fact that He sent His only son, Jesus to be the sacrifice for my sins and the sins of the world. The very fact that He did that changed my view of Him and made me realize that God cares deeply about every aspect of my life and is delighted in me when I trust Him with all things and not just the big ones.

You see, God is not the "out of reach captain of the ship" that doesn't even know that you exist so far below the deck. He is standing right next to you waiting for you to put your hand in His so that He can share the burden and steer the ship beyond the danger of rocks and reefs. He delights in having a relationship with you. He loves you more than you can comprehend, and He truly does concern Himself with every aspect of your life! My hope is for you to have an abiding relationship with Jesus Christ. Remember that the same God who spoke creation into existence knows all about you, including every thought and concern no matter how small. He knows your name and how many breaths you take each day and wants to be the one who comforts you when you are overwhelmed. Allow yourself to trust Him enough with all the details of your life. Only then will your ship be sailing in fair and calm seas. Start a conversation with Him and have a deep comfort in knowing that He cares about every detail of your life.

May God bless you as you lean into His attributes and experience the peace that surpasses all understanding. I am praying that God will become very real to you and that others will notice a change in your behavior. May God change all of us so that we display His love and glory throughout our families and neighborhoods. May He bless you today as you step out in faith. Dear friends, revival is possible as long as we take Him first.

Rely on Your Equipment

*H*AVE YOU EVER DONE any serious rock or mountain climbing? Have you had to use ropes, an ice ax, crampons, or other specialized equipment? In some cases, equipment and the proper use of this equipment is the main reason that climbers who get into trouble survive accidents that could have resulted in death. Every piece of equipment is inspected, cared for, and given the once over to make sure that it will not malfunction. Hours are spent training with the equipment to make sure that every team member knows the proper use and function of the equipment.

Have you ever thought about the equipment God has given us to lead the Christian life? He has given us everything we need to walk with Him. The tools of prayer, Bible reading, and faith offer a firm foundation and provide tremendous protection. God doesn't want us living in constant worry and anxiety. He doesn't want us cut off from the lifeline, dangling over the crevice ready to fall into an abyss with no way out. Just as a climber would never use a frayed rope; we need to make sure we are not left without resources when we face difficulties.

When I think about all the tools God has given us, I first think about prayer. Prayer is the most wonderful tool for the Christian. It's always available to us. We can pray anytime, anywhere, about anything and everything. Sometimes, prayer is all we have. I think about all the times I've been asked to pray for someone's surgery or hospital stay. I can't do a lot to heal a medical condition, but the tool of prayer can be greatly used during those times. You can pray without ceasing and even pray and beg God for help when you see no way out. He is there, and He does care. God delights when we talk to Him and admit that we need His help, direction, guidance, and wisdom. He also delights when we just take a few minutes to thank Him for everything He has given to us. Our jobs, homes, families, and friends, the beautiful creation and mostly our Savior Jesus Christ. For me, spending a few minutes praising Him gives me an immediate attitude adjustment when I'm feeling low, overwhelmed, or disappointed.

I'm sure you have already guessed that the Bible is the next piece of equipment you want in your arsenal of resources to navigate everyday life. We are so lucky to have it available to us. Many of us have multiple Bibles in our homes. Attending church and hearing preaching is a great way to get familiar with God through Bible study. My favorite way to study is to take a passage of scripture and ask myself how it applies to me. I love to pick out words and phrases and read them over and over. I also love to pick out phrases that talk about the attributes of God. You see, I discovered that the attributes of God are found everywhere in scripture. He is loving, sovereign, holy, just, all-knowing, faithful, healer, and so much more. It's always worth it to spend time memorizing scripture as well, for you never know when scripture is just what a friend or family member needs to get through a rough time.

Faith is another key attribute to move ahead gracefully in navigating life's challenges and be able to feel that continued security that only God can give. I love to read Hebrews chapter 11, which talks about faith, which is not easy to attain immediately and must be developed. Turning every aspect of our lives over to Him is very hard, but it is what He wants from us. He is trustworthy and He expects us to put our complete trust in Him. As we proceed step by step, we can learn to trust Him more. It takes time, but as we spend time praying and reading His word, it will get easier.

The Christian life is not an easy journey, but with the proper and steadfast use of the equipment available to us, we can reach the summit successfully! God wants to see your happy confident face on the top of the mountain. Commit to training with your equipment each day and step out in faith knowing that God Himself is holding the rope. He won't let you fall. He will guide every step of the way through prayer, the Bible and its scriptures, and your faith in Him!

Have a Mentor

MANY YEARS AGO, A woman told me that wise women have two things in common. They have a strong mentor in their life, and they are actively mentoring someone else. The principle is simple: receive guidance, knowledge, and wisdom from a mentor; and in turn, pass that along to the person you are mentoring. When my children were small, we lived overseas in the kingdom of Thailand. Life was very busy as we served our country in Bangkok with the American Embassy. I spent a lot of time mentoring my kids, but I lacked a strong mentor in my life.

Several years after returning to the United States, I became involved in Bible Study Fellowship (BSF). It was unlike any Bible study I had ever participated in. It would start every September and continue through the academic year for thirty weeks. They would pick a book of the Bible and go through an in-depth study of God's Word. I took my youngest son William with me, and it became his favorite place to go each week. I loved the challenge of answering the questions and attending and participating in the group discussions. William eventually started school, but I kept going and before I knew it, several years had passed and one day my leader asked me if I would like to lead a group. I was thrilled! I was also a little scared even though I knew that God would enable me. I didn't realize it, but God was going to give me a very special mentor to help guide me gracefully into leadership. God provided me with a wonderful and skilled mentor named Marcia. Marcia had been a BSF leader for several years, and she had dedicated her life and career as a teacher.

We had to commute almost an hour to the leader meetings each way. I drove and Marcia mentored me. Those discussions were a rich and cherished part of my life as she conveyed her experiences, lessons, and wisdom on being a leader and on shepherding a group. I was blessed beyond measure, and I got the best guidance I could have ever asked for. This went on for two years until Marcia moved to Hungary to become a missionary. When she moved away, it was bittersweet. I missed her terribly, but God, in His perfect timing, had equipped me to be on my own, and I succeeded beyond my own expectations!

I think for, most women, being a mentor comes more readily than having one. In my life, this has certainly been the case. I still lead a BSF group, so I continue mentoring there and plan on doing so as long as the Lord can use me. If you have a mentor in your life right now, consider yourself richly blessed. After two years in the mission field, Marcia returned home, so we are together once again and enjoying time with one another. Marcia joined my BSF group, and after one year, she was called to lead her own group again. It has been amazing to see how God orchestrated events to come full circle. Mentoring can also come in the form of exploring biographies of Christian men and women and listening to podcasts on particular issues of interest. There are many ways to enlarge your vision and learning if you don't have a person to be your mentor. Rest assured that God will make a way for you as you seek Him and ask for His will and direction.

As God challenges us in mentoring others, He does provide. Be open to being a mentor and pray for God to send you a mentor. You never know how He will answer, but He is faithful, and you can trust Him to meet your needs. He loves you and will not leave your side as you face struggles and challenges in life. May His peace give you comfort, guidance, and wisdom.

Refine Your Thinking

HAVE YOU EVER HEARD this quote? "If the enemy keeps reminding you of your past; remind him of your future." What a statement, so simple, true, and effective. So many times, the enemy has us cornered, and we get stuck in guilt and heartache, unable to move forward. If you find yourself stuck, then stick it to the enemy! God wants all of us moving forward with joy. The enemy is already defeated, and he knows it. He just wants us to think we are powerless and hopeless.

At any one time, we are either listening to the enemy or listening to God. His Holy Spirit will never lead us the wrong way. The enemy will lie to you and convince you that God's way is not the best way or the fun way. He will tell you that God wants to take things from you that make you happy. It could not be further from the truth. God wants to give you the desires of your heart. He wants to give you the best and have you experience joy and fulfillment. If you are always feeling guilty, other than godly convictions, you are listening to the lies of the enemy.

One thing I find helpful in sorting out thoughts that are lies, as opposed to godly truth, is to refine my thinking. I do this by renewing my mind in scripture on a daily basis. He promises to renew our strength by renewing our minds. Romans 12:2 says, "Do not conform to the pattern of this world but be transformed by the renewing of your mind." Then you will be able to test and approve what God's will is, His good, pleasing, and perfect will. There are so many scriptures that deal with renewing the mind. Romans 13:14, Luke 12:15, and Psalm 139:14 are all wonderful verses to remind us of who we are before the Lord. I love to keep a journal where I record everything I am thankful for, and write out some verses that will keep my mind in line with God. I encourage you to ask God, as often as necessary, for Him to be very clear in directing you. I often beg Him for help and ask Him to make His path very clear to me so that I don't miss it. When I really take Him first, He never disappoints me. You may feel challenged by the direction that He is taking you, but you can have peace about it.

Please know that God loves you more than you could possibly know. You are so special and precious to Him. He is your Protector, Shepherd, and Counselor. He is waiting now to provide you with peace, wisdom, and comfort!

Happy Christmas

I CANNOT BELIEVE THAT WE are on the doorstep of the Christmas holiday. This is really my favorite time of year. There is just something about the birth of Christ that creates a sense of wonder, joy, and well-being.

Most of us redecorate our entire house, put up a tree, and bake dozens of cookies. We participate in special events, attend parties, and do a lot of volunteer work. These are all good and worthwhile things, but sometimes, it can create unwanted stress and overwhelm. Before you know it, you may have arguments starting and become resentful that you have so much on your plate.

This year, I am going to remind myself that there is no need to "do it all." The enemy doesn't want us to enjoy Christmas and remember our Savior. He wants to stir up division and make us bitter and angry. The enemy is the author of chaos, and if I am not aware, he will put a wedge in everything I try to do.

Determine in your mind to focus on Christ in everything you do. Start each day in prayer and Bible reading. Play godly music as you clean and decorate your house. Sing Christmas carols as you bake cookies. When you start to feel overwhelmed, invite the Holy Spirit to provide comfort and direction. I have even been known to pray that God will slow down time so that I can get more done. It's not impossible for God. He can help you speed up and get more done.

Remember that God wants you to have a happy Christmas, with unity in everything you do. He wants you to share the good news of the Gospel with your friends and neighbors. Ask God to give you extra stamina to bake cookies for them and the boldness to invite them to a church service as your guest. Ask Him to remove fear and disbelief. Spend as much time as possible with Him, and then thank God for sending His son to be born in Bethlehem. Have a happy Christmas, and may God bless you!

Quiet Time

HOW DO YOU ORGANIZE your day? How do you start each day? How do you manage your personal time? Do you make your bed every morning? Do you retreat to an area of the house for coffee and quiet time? There have been many books written on this subject, and many experts in the field of education and management agree that some form of routine is necessary to optimize your productivity.

As Christians, we are challenged to put all else aside and take God first. How is that possible with the busyness of family life, work, and education? I think of the words of my wonderful husband, Jeff, who is an expert in such challenges. He says, "Don't get overwhelmed. Just break it down into small chunks!" He is so right. Nothing was ever accomplished by being discouraged from the start because you thought the task was hopelessly impossible. What does that look like for people who seem to have it all together and meet their goals?

I find that starting the night before the day begins is a key predecessor task to succeeding in getting things done. I simply take a calendar or a piece of paper and write down what I want to accomplish the next day. You don't need to prioritize or think about it too hard. Write down whatever comes to mind. Some people are very crafty with bullet journals and washi tape. If that gives you joy, do it. It is not necessary, though, and most of the time, my list is simple and in pencil. The first thing on my list is always the same. Spend time in the Word of God and pray. I make coffee and go to a special chair in my office. I look forward to that time. Sometimes my husband joins me, and that is such a blessing. The following is a list of the things I do during that time.

1. *Start and or complete any homework for a personal or group Bible study.* During the academic year, I am in BSF, so I do that work after spending a short time in prayer asking God to help me, guide me, and give me wisdom to understand what He is teaching me.

2. *Write out some verses.* Pick any number of verses and grab a notebook and write them out. Pick a shorter book of the Bible and copy it out three verses at a time (small chunks). You will be participating in an ancient tradition because the Bible was copied over and over to be preserved for future generations. As you copy out the verses, you will gain a deeper understanding of what God is saying. It is also very helpful if you are trying to memorize.

3. *Use an app.* This is especially helpful when my husband and I are having coffee together. We start the app and listen to the Bible for about fifteen minutes. There are so many good Bible apps. This is also great when you travel. Listen to Psalm 91 as you rush through the airport to get to your gate. Apps also offer Bible sleep stories and how to use verses to combat things like anxiety and depression

4. *Do a word study.* Pick a word like *suffering, joy,* or *hope.* Look up verses containing that word. Ask yourself what the passage says about the topic. Ask yourself how you can apply that to your day.

There are many other ways to use this first part of the day. The whole point is to start something. I have experienced over and over that I can get through most things on my list with joy if I start the night before, and I take God first in the morning. He will be so happy you took Him first. He will bless you by helping you get things done. He will not leave you on your own to sort things out. He wants to shoulder the burden. Let Him help you! You will be amazed at what He can accomplish.

Happy New Year

HOW DO YOU HANDLE a brand-new year? Do you think about the last year and assess goals accomplished? Do you write out resolutions and try to stick to them? Do you face the new year with no plans at all and hope that everything goes well? I'll be honest with you; I have tried to keep resolutions for years but never managed to keep them. If you find yourself with the same frustration, then what I am about to share may help you.

I ran across an email that caught my attention. It is called MY ONE WORD. Instead of making lists of what you want to accomplish, you choose one word that characterizes the kind of person you want to become. It is absolutely brilliant. Start by really searching your mind and heart. Come up with a list of traits that describe who you want to be. Have fun with it. Pray for guidance from God. Narrow it down to one word. Once you have your word, look it up in the Bible. Read as many of the verses that have that word in it. If your word is not in the Bible, look it up in the dictionary and find an alternate word. You will find one. Narrow your choice down to one verse. Memorize this verse. Write it in the pages of your calendar. Write it on a card and carry it with you. Put it on a sticky note and leave it on your bathroom mirror. Write in in the cover of your Bible, and your journal for the year. This verse will be your personal mantra for the next year. No more need for endless lists. You now have your word that will go with you and help transform you into the person that you want to become.

During times of stress, frustration, and discouragement, you just think about your word. That will bring to mind your verse, and voila, you are armed and ready to deal with any battle you may face! Your word will provoke your mind to look up and think about Him, taking your mind off the problems you are contemplating to resolve. Your verse and word will provide fortification. It's easier than pounding out endless lists of goals done under our own strength. Your chosen word has the power to transform you into the person that can accomplish those goals. It is so exciting, and results will happen! This is the power of the Holy Spirit working in you to accomplish a renewed mind and heart.

Last year, my word was strength. I can't tell you how many times God used this word to help me through a year of challenges. I managed to get physically stronger which was great, but the best part was how God taught me to trust in His strength. He worked on my mind and heart to have faith in Him and not to panic and worry over all the stressors in my life. So as you face another year, face it with one word that can transform you. As obstacles come (and they will), claim your word, take a breath, and recall your scripture. You are now armed and ready to face any challenge. I think you will enjoy this method and different ways to start the year. It is so exciting to see what God has for you. May your relationship with Him grow closer and more real as you lean into Him and His word. I believe that He is so pleased when we trust Him and depend on Him. May God richly bless you as He brings clarity, wisdom, and peace to your life.

How Is Your Compassion

> Rejoicing in hope; patient in tribulation;
> continuing instant in prayer.
> —Romans 12:12.

I RECENTLY CARED FOR A young woman who was struggling with her health. She had made some really bad choices to abuse drugs and alcohol, which left her with permanent damage to her brain and other vital organs. She really suffered from terrible symptoms. Her very disturbing and disruptive behavior included yelling, swearing, agitation, and anxiety. She was absolutely inconsolable. Calming medications had very little effect. She was a challenge to care for, and medical interventions were not effective.

After a period of several days, she finally had some visitors. A distant cousin and his family had traveled over three thousand miles to see her. I could tell right away that this was not your average family. Both husband and wife were pleasant and courteous and had three very well-behaved children with them. I gave a brief report to the wife and helped them put on their gowns and gloves before entering the room. The husband began to speak to his cousin, but his voice was barely audible or perceptible because he was suffering from throat cancer. His wife explained to me that he was a pastor.

This family spent a lot of time in the room. They were loving, kind, and patient. They prayed for her out loud and sang many uplifting hymns at the bedside. The effect of this was miraculous. She calmed down and finally rested for the first time in three days. It was such a joy and privilege to see the Holy Spirit work through this wonderful family.

As they were preparing to leave, the wife pulled me aside and said, "Do you need prayer for anything?" Her countenance was so sweet and genuine that it threw me off guard for a moment. She was completely sincere. Her question was based on nothing other than God's own love. I have never encountered anything like this from a stranger. What a testament for the Lord. After all, she had every right to be stressed. Her husband had cancer. That didn't stop this lady. She had her eyes on Jesus and I could tell that she was overflowing with His love.

What stuck with me about this encounter was this family's conviction to show God's love. No judgment, no agenda. No impatience nor falsehood. I had to ask myself, am I like this? Am I that sincere? Am I that bold? Are my motivations pure? I was very convinced that I need to work on being more like Jesus.

Take time to step out and encourage someone this week. You never know the impact you will have. Pray for God's love to flow through you!

The Good Shepherd

HAVE YOU EVER FELT like you were so overloaded with tasks that you might drown in stress? Sometimes I have had so much stress I felt frozen in time and could not breathe. I think everyone has had a time or two when you felt like one more thing would push you under with no way to dig yourself out. For me, this situation almost always comes up at work. It is standard practice at any time to be pulled in so many different directions that I feel the only answer is to literally clone myself! I've been meditating on ways that God provides order, peace, emotional stability, and joy even in the midst of incredible overwhelm.

Genesis 2:7 says, "And the LORD God formed man of the dust of the ground and breathed into his nostrils the breath of life and the man became a living soul." Now, there is no life without breath. Have you ever seen kids hold their breath when they get anxious or have a tantrum? As adults, we do the same thing. What we all need when under stress is a little breath. Oxygen fuels muscles and give clarity to your brain, it will cause you to focus off the stress ahead of you and help you categorize and prioritize what to do next. So next time you are about ready to burst, breathe. Here is how I do it:

1. Breathe deeply through your nose and say, "One."
2. Breathe out through your mouth and say, "Two." Repeat as often as is needed throughout the day.

First Corinthians 14:40 says, "And let all things be done decently and in order."

After you take a few deep breaths, think about what has to be done first. Try to think about creating space between you and the huge pile of work. In your space, you have room to breathe, move, and make decisions about what to do first. As you categorize and prioritize, that space will get bigger, and you will start to feel more in command of the situation. You don't want to get stuck here, just pick one thing and do it, and then you can move on to the next.

John 10:11 says, "I am the good shepherd, the shepherd giveth his life for his sheep." At this stage, you may be on your way to gaining the upper hand in the battle of overwhelm. If you are not, then I find it helpful to remind myself of John chapter 10, The Good Shepherd. This chapter is packed full of compassion, mercy, and truth. I recently found out that sheep have a hard time getting up if they fall over. If they are down for more than about forty-five minutes, they will die of suffocation. That is why the shepherd is so key. He is the lifeline for the flock. He leads them, feeds and waters them, fights off wolves, gives them rest in the pen, and binds any wounds that they have. When they get lost, he searches for them and brings them back to the flock. I cannot think of a better way to combat overwhelm then to think about Jesus the Good Shepherd. He is always there, leading the way to peace, rest, and joy.

Next time you feel overwhelmed, remember to breathe, create space and organization, and allow the Good Shepherd to lead you into a peaceful pasture. You can trust Him to help you have joy in the most difficult circumstances.

When We Don't Obey

MANY YEARS AGO, I had a patient that was very near death. She had multiorgan failure that meant there was nothing doctors could do to save her life. She looked very bad. The doctor came in every day with a smile on his face and a big dose of hope for the family. He said, "She is looking really good, better than yesterday." This comment made me burn inside because I knew it was a lie. She would not get better. It was unfair of him to give the family hope where there was none. As I cared for her throughout my shift, the Holy Spirit began to speak to me. I began to feel convicted about the eternity that she would be facing. God was telling me that I should share the Gospel with her and do it soon. She had four or five family members at the bedside. I knew they needed to hear the Good News too. At that time, I made a plan to go home after my shift was over, change clothes and come back to share the Gospel with her and her family. As I made this decision, I started to become gripped with fear. I went home that night and never came back. I disobeyed God's voice and discovered during my next shift that she had passed away. I had missed my opportunity!

Fear and disbelief will always stifle God's Good News. I rationalized that if I came back, I could get fired. I convinced myself that it was too scary. I will never forget the time that I disobeyed His voice. Since that day I have depended on God to help me deliver His good news. I don't let fear and disbelief grip me into inaction. I grieve for that lady and her family. I made a mistake, and I have become determined to not do that again.

When you feel the nudge from the Holy Spirit to share the Gospel, expect some opposition from the enemy. Stop and ask God to help you carry out His work with confidence and peace. He will help you. He is the one who does the saving. Obeying His voice is the best thing you can do. Maybe you have never shared the Gospel and the thought of it sends you reeling into a panic. You are not alone; I've been there. Start with one thing. Pray that God gives you a heart for the lost. Just pray. That's all you need to do. Then pray that God brings you just one person that is ready to hear the message. Trust Him to give you boldness to share. It is so easy to brush off and miss opportunities. Obedience has so many benefits. Trust God to give you the ability to carry out His work. He will deliver and not disappoint.

I pray that you will put Him to the test and let Him help you with difficult things. He is able and we are not. Every day, I have had to live with my decision to not share when God was directing me to. I learned a hard lesson that day, and it has changed me forever. May God bless you richly as you step out in faith to obey Him. He loves you more than you could imagine. He is gracious to forgive and mighty to save!

Thanking God for Prayers That Took Years

Hear my cry, O God: attend unto my prayer
from all the end of the earth will I cry
unto thee, when my heart is overwhelmed:
lead me to the rock that is higher than
I. For thou hast been a shelter for me,
and a strong tower from the enemy.
—Psalm 61:1–3

PRAYER IS THE MOST wonderful tool for the Christian. Many times, we pray and get immediate answers. Other times the answer is a complete surprise. Sometimes we get no answer. Sometimes the problem is so complex and chronic that we don't see answers for months or even years. What do you do when you don't see answers? What if you are stuck in the miry clay of difficulty and you don't see any way out? If you are in that situation, then I hope the story I am about to tell you will encourage you.

Several weeks ago, I started preparing for our oldest son's graduation from high school. I searched through pictures to show his progression from infancy to adulthood. It was a difficult task because our charter school only allowed ten photos. My process was slow because as I made my way through the photos, I stopped to look at each one and reminisced about the circumstances that surrounded that moment in time.

Our son Andrew struggled with behavior and learning difficulties his entire life. He was diagnosed with many problems, but it was all eventually settled on Asperger's syndrome. It challenged him socially, academically, psychologically, and physically. I was completely overwhelmed during his early years. His behavior seemed impossible to control even with strict and sound parenting skills. I began to get very frustrated and angry and even began to blame myself for what I could have done to cause all these problems. Many times, I only had the resource of prayer to deal with the distress and dysfunction of it all. I put Andrew into God's hands and entrusted his care and outcomes to Him. I begged God to intervene and heal him. God was working in the background, but our whole family suffered the consequences of Andrew's out-of-control behavior and learning disabilities. My marriage was stressful Andrew's younger brother was afraid of him. Things were going downhill fast. Many times, I didn't know how I would survive the day, or even the next five minutes.

I remember hearing about a boarding school in England that took care of children like Andrew. I started calculating how many double shifts I would have to work to send him there. At this point, I was the default person to deal with Andrew. No one else could take him on. As I spent more and more time with him, I had less time for his younger brother. Poor young William was ignored by me because Andrew was a full-time job. God began teaching me that I had to become Andrew's coach. I sought out counsel through books and experts in the field. I fervently prayed and prayed. Andrew got kicked out of junior church for drawing a body part on the whiteboard. I taught three-year-olds during that time, and my husband was deployed to Southwest Asia during the Iraqi War, so I had no choice but to bring him into the class with me. I had Andrew help me teach the three-year-olds, and with expertise and patience, he taught them, and they listened. They sat still and paid attention to him. God began unraveling a plan and for the first time I saw hope.

Schooling had its own set of challenges. I really felt that Andrew should attend school. We tried Christian school, public school, and specialized private school. He kept getting expelled. One school literally lost him on the first day. I went to pick him up and no one could find him! Another school let him sit in his wet jeans for two hours because they wouldn't let him go to the bathroom. Another school said that the students were so stressed by his presence that they were going to the nurse's office to ask for medication to calm them down. At this point, with a long and upsetting trial of past failures, I decided to homeschool. I was stepping into unknown territory and had no support. I prayed and prayed and prayed again for God's help. By seventh grade Andrew was doing math at the first-grade level. He could barely write a sentence. He was anxious and depressed. He declared himself an atheist. My husband wept at the announcement. Our whole family was stunned. Andrew declined into a very dark existence. I kept praying; I prayed that God would send people to me who could help us. We insisted that Andrew attend church with us, but I had to pinch him over and over to keep him awake during services.

I begged God to help me. I spent time on my knees crying my eyes out before the Almighty God in heaven for answers, wisdom, and direction. Years were passing by, and it seemed things just got worse. My husband began to explore about what would happen with Andrew if we both passed away. We had grave concerns about Andrew's future.

We completed ninth grade with little success. Finally, we had a breakthrough as God led me to a person who could test him and make a plan to help. We ended up repeating ninth grade using different strategies and specialized tutors that made a difference. High school became a full-time job, evaluating every step of the way. A huge breakthrough came when I gave up on making Andrew write papers by hand. Once I unleashed him on the computer, he wrote beautiful papers. Stress and anxiety began to decrease, and progress was seen. Finally, Andrew graduated from high school as the class valedictorian and delivered the valedictorian speech so eloquently and confidently. We then put a massive effort into ACT prep. He was accepted into Azusa Pacific University and graduated with a degree in criminal justice with a minor in psychology. Andrew will be getting married next month. He works full time in health care, managing an entire office on his own!

I have no doubt that God never left our side, even in the darkest days. I have no doubt we could have had a very different outcome had it not been for His great intervention and love for us. Whatever struggle you face, He is trustworthy. He is able. In the end, Andrew's growth and miraculous metamorphosis is a testimony to His steadfast love and amazing power to transform anyone!

"Trust in Him at all times: ye people, pour out your heart before him: God is a refuge for us" (Psalm 62:8).

The 21-Day Fix

I JUST COMPLETED A DIET and workout regime called "The 21 Day Fix." The creator of this plan claims that if you adhere to her guidelines for twenty-one days you will be rewarded with a healthy, fit body. She starts each day with a little mantra that says, "If you want to stop starting over, then you have to stop quitting." I have lost the same pounds over and over because I gave up on myself and quit. I've had to start over a number of times. Unfortunately, this cycle creates a feeling of failure, followed by despair and lack of confidence and hope. It's such a bad feeling to give up on yourself. You lose momentum, get stuck, and start to realize that you missed the opportunity for success. Unfortunately, sometimes friends and family members give up on you because they see your failure and lack of self-control. It's hard for them to believe in someone who doesn't even believe in themselves. If you find yourself in a situation like this, I have some good news for you. You are not alone.

Did you know that no matter how much you give up, God never gives up on you. He is always there, just a whisper of a prayer away, waiting for you to take His hand and lead you into a high tower above all the muck and mire. There are dozens of Bible promises that assure us that God is near, and that He cares. In Joshua 1:5, He promises not to fail us. He commands us to be strong and promises to give us strength. Psalm 46:1 reminds us that "He is our refuge." He will not leave us to deal with trouble ourselves, He promises to help us through it. Matthew 28:20 promises us that He is ever present with us to the end of time. Romans 8:38 promises that there is no trial or amount of persecution that can separate us from the love of God. The entire chapter of Romans 8 is a testament to the fact that He bolsters us up by the mighty and powerful love of Christ. We are His adopted children! How fantastic is that!

With all these promises and instruction on how to receive them, there is really no reason to give up on ourselves. One thing is certain: He cannot and will not give up on you. May you feel the truth of His presence and know that He will help you overcome any obstacle. You are more than a conqueror, not a failure. God bless you.

The Cure

AS MANY OF YOU know, I am a registered nurse, and I've worked to care for hundreds of patients over the last three decades. It has always struck me that nurses administer the cure for disease and infection. Doctors assess and diagnose the problem. They order medication to alleviate pain and hopefully cure the disease. It is always the nurse however who administers the cure. Most patients are willing to do whatever it takes to alleviate their pain and cure the ailment. They will swallow down foul elixirs and choke down enormous horse pills in order to get out of the hospital and get home.

If you are a Christian, you have the cure for the soul. You know the truth that sets the captive free. You know the Gospel, the good news about eternal life. Have you ever shared the cure?

Many times, at the hospital I've taken care of patients who don't want my help. They yell, try to hit me, and throw their pills at the door. It was during one of these challenges that got me thinking. If I had a cure for any disease, would I share it with everyone? Try to imagine that your patient is a terrorist. Another patient sells drugs. Another traffics children in the sex trade. You have the cure for their disease. It's in your pocket. You just have to give it to them. Maybe you are hesitating. After all, is it fair that such a deplorable criminal gets the cure? Shouldn't the cure be saved for those who are more deserving? Like the father of two young children who has a brain tumor, or a child who has leukemia.

When Jesus came, He came for the sick, and weak. He came for sinners. He came for the worst of sinners. God loves everyone, and

Jesus paid the price for all to be freed from sin and have a permanent relationship with Him. It's not for me to judge who gets the cure. God is the only one qualified to judge us. God promises to make all wrongs right. To make the crooked way straight. All we need to do is share the message of salvation with as many people as we can. Don't worry about what they have done. Just share the cure. God will take care of the rest.

Spend a few minutes thanking God for the person who shared the Gospel with you. I am so glad no one judged me, thinking I don't deserve to hear the message. I am so glad they looked past all my faults and told me how to get saved. I challenge you to pray for God to send you just one person to share the Gospel with. There is nothing sweeter than seeing someone come alive and truly experience the freedom in God's love. May you feel His blessing and joy as you abide in His love. May you be strengthened and encouraged as you obey the prompting of the Holy Spirit. He will not fail you. God bless you!

The Thankfulness Jar

HAVE YOU EVER HEARD of a thankfulness jar? It's really easy to create one. Just take any clear glass jar, place it in a space in your home that gets some activity and traffic, and place a pencil and a few sticky notes by it. Let everyone know that every time they walk by the jar, they should write something they are thankful for and place it inside. It's that simple. In the past, we have done this starting November 1 and then opened and read all the notes on Thanksgiving Day.

Being thankful should never be underestimated. When you express gratitude, you receive far more than you give. There are even studies that claim being thankful has health benefits such as improved immunity, better moods, and more restful REM sleep quality. It has even been shown to improve self-esteem, decrease anxiety and depression, and to help you have a more positive outlook on life. Gratitude has even been shown to light up the portions of the brain that create the happy chemicals like serotonin and dopamine. The practice of being thankful is also deeply embedded in the Word of God. First Thessalonians 5:16–18 says, "Rejoice always, pray continually, give thanks in all circumstances for this is God's will for you in Christ Jesus." Psalm 103:1–4 talks about praising God from your innermost being. James 1–17 reminds us that all good gifts come from the Father. Psalm 95:1–5 encourages us to sing for joy unto the Lord and bow down before Him in thanksgiving.

One last thing about thankfulness. There is a really special positive result to be had if someone thanks you for something. It's kind of like supersizing all the benefits. When was the last time someone wrote you a thank you note? Do you remember how it made you feel? It probably stirred up some really happy emotions. So don't forget to name names when you write your notes for your jar. If your son took out the trash, write it. If your husband cleaned out the garage, write it. If your wife vacuumed the entire house and cooked a full three course meal, write it! When they pull those notes out of the jar their hearts will sing.

I pray that you will take the time to set up your thankfulness jar. It's an activity that benefits everyone. May God richly bless you and may you feel His love today.

We All Need a Coach

PERHAPS SOME OF YOU played team sports and had a coach for soccer or swimming. If so, have you ever had a personal coaching session? Maybe you had a love-hate relationship with your coach. I have heard some coaches say, "I love you enough to let you hate me." In other words, they know the only way to victory is to push you to the breaking point and let you hate them a little bit for the goal of success.

In our Christian life, we have a coach. He is the person of the *Holy Spirit*. He is our helper, counselor, and comforter. I find that I need to be meeting with Him each day for workouts, instructions, directions, and drills. If I don't show up for training, I end up huffing and puffing my way through the day in a weak and deconditioned state. The Holy Spirit is our personal coach to help us navigate the battleground of life. He will arm us with the weapons to have victory over stress, depression, anxiety, and despair. He will guide you to success, but you have to show up for training.

I want to encourage you to take every opportunity this week to pray, memorize scripture, study your Bible, and sing songs of praise to Him. He will have you fit and ready to face whatever battle is around the next corner. I have personally found that every effort into

Bible memorization pays huge dividends. It is a powerful tool to keep you on track and fight the enemy.

May God richly bless you as you enter into a deeper and more fulfilling relationship with Him. May you find victory in each battle that you face. He loves you and will not leave your side (Colossians 3:16–17).

My Worth Is Not in What I Own

EVERY TIME THE FALL season arrives, I have wonderful memories of colored leaves, pumpkins, and apple cider. It also makes me think about school. I was always quite nervous about school starting. I was a very shy girl and all the extra activity and demands made me anxious and extremely nervous. I got anxious about other things too because it highlighted the fact that our family had trouble making ends meet. Mom would sew our clothes for the school year, and my sister Nancy and I would get two dresses and one hand-knit cardigan. The dresses were short-sleeved and knee-length so that it would fit us until school let out in June. Nancy and I brought sack lunches from home which consisted of a peanut butter sandwich and an apple. Sometimes we would be delighted and excited that Mom had made cookies to put in our lunch.

Nancy and I were not immediately aware that money was really tight in our family. By the time we reached high school, we could see that our clothes and food were a lot different than the other girls. Sometimes we were made fun of because we wore the same clothes all the time. I began to develop a sense of shame and started to believe that something was wrong with me. I began to dream about having money for school lunches and store-bought clothes.

I did not know the Lord then, and I didn't understand that my self-worth should be coming from Him. Since that time, I have learned that if I try to be like someone else, I rob myself of the blessing that God has for me. I put myself in a perpetual state of comparison and heartache.

The Bible says I am fearfully and wonderfully made. There is only one of me. God has a special job that only I can do. Why should I constantly compare myself with others and desire their life over my own? I certainly don't want to miss my calling and special purpose.

Once I realized that I needed to stop looking sideways and look up instead, I realized that my Savior was there waiting to embrace me and remind me of how special, beautiful, and unique I was. This is where true freedom comes from. Asking Him to reveal His true purpose for me was the best thing I ever did, and He has blessed me more than I could even imagine. I have so much to be thankful for, and I have never had need for anything. He always provides.

Please know that you are loved more than you know. Not one of your personal heartbeats escapes His notice. He cares about all your struggles, concerns, and disappointments. Call out to Him; He is waiting for you.

Alienation

HAVE YOU EVER FELT alone, alienated, empty, and upset? These feelings are part of human life, but I believe that the sense of alienation is even more prevalent than ever before. You may feel alienated at work, or when you are in public, or even when you are with friends and family members. If you feel alienated, then I have some good news for you.

If you are a Christian, there is no reason to feel alienated. God never lets you stand alone, dealing with all the pressures of the world by yourself. He wants you to share every detail of your life with Him and trust Him. He wants to bear the burden of all your fears and doubts. He wants you to depend on Him completely. Some of the scariest times I've endured were the ones where I left God out of the picture. What a lonely place to be—without God and without any hope or security. If you find yourself in this situation, call on God. He will not delay in giving you some relief. Once He takes control, you will gain a firmer footing and you will be assured of an outcome that displays His perfect will.

In studying through the scriptures, I came up with six truths to focus on.

1. *John 1:12*. Remember that you are a child of the King. You are His creation, and He loves you. The King will not let you become separated from Him. He will guard you and fight your battles. You are not alone.

2. *John 3:16.* You are greatly loved with an undying love. He paid for your life with His own.
3. *Psalm 139:13.* He knows you. You are not a stranger. He knew you before you were born.
4. *Ephesians 1:11.* He has a job that only you can do. It is unique and no one else can do it.
5. *Psalm 139:7–10.* He is always with you.
6. *Ephesians 1 :13.* He has sealed you with His spirit. You will never be taken or separated from Him.

Just remember that no matter how tough it gets, He is at your side. He will not leave you. He is fighting for you, and He loves you. It doesn't get much better than that. Share these verses this week with a friend who needs encouragement.

How to Survive a Rough Day

WHEN YOU HAVE A rough day, what do you turn to? Chocolate, chips, a movie marathon? Maybe all three. We have all had rough days. With kids, it's pretty much guaranteed. Life gets so busy and tempers flare. I have found that if I have a few things in my spiritual toolbox, I can make it through the most challenging circumstances.

The following six points are notes from a sermon by Dr. Don Sisk. Dr. Sisk is one of the wisest men I know, and no matter what he is going through, he always has a big smile on his face. He has perfected the art of forgiveness and has so much to say about the Christian walk that I wanted to include it here for you.

1. *Be thankful.* Take a minute and right out five things that you are thankful for. This takes the focus off the current moment and puts it on God where it belongs. Read some of the Psalms. Psalm 91 is particularly comforting.
2. *Forgive* the ones who are messing up your day. Refuse to retaliate (Luke 6:37).
3. *Encourage* others who are struggling (Luke 23:43).
4. *Take your difficult questions to the Lord.* Pour your heart out Him like David did in so many of the Psalms (Psalm 140:1).

5. *Make your needs known* so that others can pray for you (Philippians 1:3–4).
6. *Have faith and commit all things to God.* Anything I commit to the Lord is something that I can stop worrying about.

I pray that these verses and truths will help you survive even the worst of days. May God's Words encourage you, comfort you, and give you peace.

The Enemy

HAVE YOU EVER HEARD this quote? If the enemy keeps reminding you of your past, remind him of your future. What a statement, so simple, true, and effective. So many times, the enemy has us cornered, and we get stuck in guilt and heartache, unable to move forward. If you find yourself stuck, then stick it to the enemy. God wants all of us moving forward with joy. The enemy is already defeated, and he knows it. He just wants us to think we are powerless and hopeless.

At any one time, we are either listening to the enemy or listening to God. His Holy Spirit will never lead us the wrong way. The enemy will lie to you and convince you that God's way is not the best way or the fun way. He will tell you that God wants to take things from you that make you happy. It could not be further from the truth. God wants to give you the desires of your heart. He wants to give you the best and have you experience joy and fulfillment. If you are always feeling guilty, other than godly convictions, you are listening to the lies of the enemy.

One thing I find helpful in sorting out thoughts that are lies, as opposed to godly truth, is to refine my thinking. I do this by renewing my mind in scripture on a daily basis. He promises to renew our strength by renewing our minds. Romans 12:2 says, "Do not conform to the pattern of this world, but be transformed by the renewing of your mind." Then you will be able to test and approve what God's will is, his good, pleasing, and perfect will. There are so many scriptures that deal with renewing the mind. Romans 13:14,

Luke 12:15, and Psalm 139:14 are wonderful verses to remind us of who we are before the Lord. I love to keep a journal where I record everything, I am thankful for and write out some verses that will keep my mind in line with God. I encourage you to ask God, as often as necessary, for Him to be very clear in directing you. I often beg Him for help and ask Him to make His path very clear to me so that I don't miss it. When I really take Him first, He never disappoints me. You may feel challenged by the direction that He is taking you, but you can have peace about it.

Please know that God loves you more than you could possibly know. You are so special and precious to Him. He is your protector, Shepherd, and Counselor. He is waiting now to provide you with peace, wisdom, and comfort.

Divine Appointment

I HAVE BEEN FORTUNATE ENOUGH to attend a church that has a strong emphasis on sharing the Gospel. Classes are offered that teach how to share your faith, and you have the opportunity to partner up with an experienced person who can help. Memorizing verses from Romans was something I decided to do. I did not know it at the time, but I was being trained for a divine appointment. God would have me share my faith with someone who desperately needed to hear the good news and make a decision that would have eternal consequences.

I met a young woman at work. June was in her early thirties. She was a nurse like me, and she worked the night shift. She was a single mother of a delightful three-year-old boy. I would see her for handoff report at work. Eventually, I did not see her anymore, and months went by. I was thrilled to see her come into work one night, and I asked her how she was. She told me that she had severe stomach pains and ended up in the emergency room. They did a scan, and she was found to have stage 4 colon cancer. She seemed unphased, but I knew she was terrified inside. I could hardly believe that this had happened to her. She was so young and vibrant. I began to pray for her because a diagnosis like that had a grave prognosis.

One Sunday, while sitting in church, I felt a distinct pressure in the middle of my chest. I could hear a "still, small voice" telling me that I needed to visit June and to do it soon. God's message was very clear. I needed to share the Gospel with her because she didn't have long to live. I knew what I needed to do. It turned out that she had been hospitalized on the unit where we both worked. She was gravely ill. I knew I had to visit her that week. I had decided I would go see her after Bible study on Wednesday morning. My Bible study group was called BSF. I had been attending Bible Study Fellowship for years. As we were finishing up our study that morning, I asked a few of the ladies to pray for me after I explained to them what I would be doing. They prayed for me right at that moment and said they would continue to pray. This gave me a sense of confidence and calm as I drove to the hospital.

Oddly enough, God prompted me to stop and buy doughnuts on the way. I made the familiar walk up to my unit on the third floor and found her room. Her nurse that day was another church member. She shared with me later that she wanted to share the Gospel with June, but when she saw me come around the corner, she knew that God had given me a divine appointment. She would pray as I shared. The climate in the room was a little stressed. June's father and boyfriend were there. Her father was very rough, annoyed, and unfriendly. He warmed a little after I handed him the doughnuts. I've never been one for small talk, but I became a smiling, chatty person that day. I knew I had to speak with June alone. As I chatted, I prayed they would leave. Eventually, they both left to pick up June's son from school. I knew this was the opportunity I was looking for. I asked June if she knew where she would go if she were to pass away. She immediately broke into tears and said she didn't know. She said she had been taught that she got sick because she was sinful and did not have enough faith in God to make her well. Everything she was going through, the sickness, the pain, and the stress was her fault. I was so heartbroken about the burden she was under. I immediately shared with her that Jesus loved her so much that He died for her sins. He was waiting, willing and able to forgive her and promise her a place in heaven with Him for an eternity. She prayed to Him to forgive her sins and asked Him to be her Savior. After she prayed, she rolled over onto her back and her face showed peace, relief, and light! In just twenty-four hours she was in a coma, and in four days, she slipped into eternity with Jesus.

God says, the fields are white with harvest, but the laborers are few. I am so glad that I was prepared for this divine appointment with June. I am sure that God has a divine appointment for each and every one of us. Prepare yourself ahead of time by memorizing the Romans Road. Practice sharing the Gospel with other believers. Team up with others in your church who can mentor you through the process. That way, when God calls you to your own divine appointment, you are ready to carry out a mission with eternal consequences. You will be so glad you did.

This list of Bible verses known as the Romans Road allowed me to share the pathway to salvation for June, and it is a clear way to lead someone to the saving grace of Jesus Christ:

The Romans Road

For all have sinned and come short of the glory of God. (Romans 3:23)

For the wages of sin is death: but the gift of God is eternal life through Jesus Christ our Lord. (Romans 6:23)

But God commendeth His love towards us, in that, while we were yet sinners, Christ died for us. (Romans 5 :8)

For whosoever shall call upon the name of the Lord shall be saved. (Romans 10:13)

Betrayal

AS I'VE BEEN STUDYING through the Gospel of John, I found myself lingering on the section where Judas betrayed Jesus. I became perplexed how someone that close to the Savior would betray Him. Perhaps you have wondered the same thing, why would someone who had spent three and a half years in a front row seat of the greatest man that ever lived turn his back on Him and betray Him? I decided that it would be helpful to study this section a little deeper and trust God for answers and insight.

Have you ever been betrayed? I think most people have been. Sometimes more than once, and in some cases a repeated betrayal occurs. We have all experienced that feeling of shock and upset when a friend, relative, teacher, child, or parent betrays us. Sometimes these things can be resolved, but in some cases, the whole matter is out of your control, and you must bear the consequences and depend on God for help and comfort.

As John writes in his gospel, he reveals the source of the betrayal. John 13:27 says, "And after the sop, Satan entered into him." Remember that your friends and family are not your enemy, but Satan is. He is the great divider and loves to sow discord. Instead of choosing Jesus, Judas chose the world and allowed Satan to control all of his actions. The good news is that if you are saved, you cannot be taken over or be inhabited by the enemy. We can, however, be swayed and tempted to cause division. Betrayal hurts, stings, breaks hearts, and causes incredible pain and emotional anguish. The source is always the enemy. Whenever and wherever I see division,

I ask myself if I am stirring up division. What are my thoughts and actions? When arguments start, I try to take a breath and remember that this is not from God. I try very hard to stop, observe, pray, and proceed with love and understanding. If needed I will accept blame and make every attempt to move on. God will make a way of escape and restore order where needed.

How did Jesus handle this betrayal? He was not offended, He did not react in anger or upset, He just dismissed him. Don't forget that Jesus had just washed Judas's feet. I am convinced that Jesus was so in tune with His Father's will that His focus remained pure. He did not deviate; His goal was obedience. What are we to do when we face betrayal or participate in betrayal? We look up and focus our eyes on Jesus. We pray to be filled with the Holy Spirit. We ask Him for clarity, wisdom, guidance, and love. We choose to obey His will and defer our own. We choose to stay in the light and not live in darkness.

As we all walk through this life, let me remind you of John 14:18: "I will not leave you comfortless: I will come to you." Isn't it nice to know that we have a friend who stays by us and never leaves? He is the source of all light, forgiveness, and grace. His love endures forever! May you stay near to Him in the coming days and depend on Him for direction, peace, and hope. God bless you!

He Sets You High on a Rock

*T*IME GOES WAY TOO fast sometimes. Seasons come and go; there are weddings, graduations, vacations, and birthdays. Time marches on no matter how busy we are. It is hard for us to keep step when we are involved in day-to-day life. One season gradually folds into the next, and before we know it, another year has passed.

I get so excited about reading the Bible. It's an anchor and constant in my life. It's alive and dynamic like the waves of the ocean. The words rise up off the page just like a wave and never stops. It keeps pouring over and over getting wrapped up in my thoughts as it lands on the shore and reaches back to get swallowed up and cast back out. Over and over, it moves in and out of my mind and heart. The word can carry you to that secret destination. The place where God wants you to be. If you ride it out, He will take you to a peaceful shore. Psalm 61:2 says, "From the end of the earth will I cry unto thee, when my heart is overwhelmed: lead me to the rock that is higher than I."

The phrase "higher than I" really spoke to me. When we are struggling and stressed, when we are overwhelmed and discouraged, we feel stuck in a pit. We need someone to pull us out. God, in His mercy, stretches out His hand and will lead us to a mountaintop where we have the advantage of the high ground. Soldiers in battle always want the high ground. The advantages are numerous. They can see for miles and spot the enemy approaching. It is harder for the enemy to reach you if they have to climb up to get you. The high ground offers opportunity to reload a weapon and take time for nourishment. If we get too busy, we may be spending too much time away from God and we may slip into a ravine. We no longer have the high ground, and we may succumb to the enemy. If you are there, take a breath, let Him pull you out and put you on a high place. You may have to say no to a few requests, but restoration comes when we spend time with Him. He doesn't expect you to fight battles alone from a pit where the enemy has the advantage. He wants to protect you and place you high up in safety and security.

Remember, there is no need to dwell in the valley if you are a Christian, start each day with an outstretched hand toward the One who can lead you to a place that is "higher than I."

God Is a God of Order

HAVE YOU RAISED A teenager? The word "order" does not exist for them. Chaos and mess is their theme—the more, the better. I honestly do not know how they can function amidst all that mess. They lose things because it is buried under a pile. There are smells of dirty socks and tennis shoes. They never make their bed or put anything away.

I don't know about you, but I am a lot happier when things are in order. I am more productive because I spend less time searching for things. I make lists and try to clean as I go when I cook dinner. No matter how tired I am, I make an effort to organize my office a little so that when I wake up in the morning I can retreat with my coffee to a place of tranquility and calm. My office has become the favorite room in the house because it's cozy, orderly, and clean. Everyone wants to spend time there. It's where I start my day with the Lord, and it feels safe to me. There is always an open Bible. I also play an audio Bible to help me memorize scripture. Sometimes I pray on my knees there and reflect on how much Jesus loves me.

Psalm 119:133 says, "Order my steps in thy word: and let not any iniquity have dominion over me." God wants us to have order on our Bible and prayer time too. I have been doing a Bible study out of a book by Debbie Alsdorf. She suggests you take a personal inventory of yourself and organize a prayer list. If the same issues keep coming up and bothering you over and over, following her method just might help.

1. Make a list of all the things you don't like about yourself. Be specific.
2. Go through the list and put a checkmark on those things that cannot be changed. These things will need to be committed to God.
3. Make a second list of everything that did not have a check mark. These are the things that can be changed. This will become your new target list. This list will become the focus of part of your prayer time.

After I did this exercise, I realized I was spending too much time and energy on things that cannot be changed. I also realized that I needed to submit more to God's power. If I was going to make progress on the target list (things that could be changed) I would have to make a reasonable plan and stick to it with God's help, wisdom, and guidance.

I hope you will try this little exercise. I also hope that all of you have even a very small space where you can meditate on God's Word and pray. If you don't have one, search for a place where you can create your own prayer closet. You never know, there may be others who desire to spend time there too.

Don't forget how much God loves you. He desires to spend time with you. Even if you don't know what to pray, He understands your struggles and the desire of your heart. He will not leave you on your own to struggle. He is always available to provide rest, peace, and comfort. God bless you.

Hummingbirds

I DON'T KNOW ABOUT YOU, BUT I get so excited about God's creatures. The amazing diversity and beauty of nature and the animal kingdom are mind-boggling. I can watch them for hours. I'm especially amazed by the variety of birds. The colors of their feathers almost show the glory of the Lord, and their behaviors truly amaze me. I get particularly excited when I see a hummingbird. They are so delightful, flitting from flower to flower and feasting off the nectar. I decided to put up a feeder. At 6:00 a.m. every morning, several little hummers would fly around the feeder and come in for a landing to feed. Some were plain and brown, but others had bright pink necks, and some had iridescent green feathers. Each one seemed to have its own particular feeding pattern. Some would relax and land on the feeder to drink. Others were more energetic and acrobatic, feeding while hovering. Sometimes they seemed to be chasing each other, making chattering noises and competing for the feeder. Days and months went by, and I could count on my little friends to arrive at 6:00 a.m. I realized that this was a gift from God who sent them for me to delight in. Each time I saw them, I thought about God. He created them, and He took care of them. They didn't have to worry. God would watch over them.

I learned a few lessons by watching these little nimble creatures. God was reminding me of the importance of early morning feeding. Just as the little hummers came in for a landing on the feeder, I needed to start each day feeding on the Word of God. Hummingbirds need frequent high-quality feedings. We need the same. If we don't start each day in the Word of God, we will be running on empty. He is waiting for us to fill up each day with His words, truths, and doctrines. God takes care of the birds. Matthew 6:26 says, "Look at the birds of the air, they neither sow nor reap, nor gather into barns, yet your heavenly father feeds them." Birds are our example to place our faith and dependence on God alone. God wants to relieve us of our constant fear and worry and replace it with confidence and trust. How wonderful that He uses His creation to remind us of these truths. Lastly, I learned that each little bird had its own habits, markings, feather colors, and feeding style. God created all of us with our own unique and wonderful personality and learning style. Seek God in the way that works for you. Pray for a plan of how to do your own Bible study. Seek God in prayer. Determine how you will start each day. We are so lucky to have dozens of different modalities for quiet time. I use a combination of apps (I love Dwell and Abide) along with more traditional Bible reading programs and Bible studies like BSF. There is something for everyone. Figure out the unique style that will work for you. Ask God to help you. He promises not to leave you alone to take care of yourself. He will provide.

I hope that you will find encouragement and guidance from God by looking at His creation. He has left us a beautiful gift to enjoy and steward. I pray that you will discover your unique style of Bible study and start each day feasting and abiding with Him. The next time you see a bird, remember that God is providing for and protecting it. You are important to Him, and He is waiting with outstretched hand to lead you into your future without fear and anxiety. I am praying for you as you trust in Him.

Do Demons Really Exist?

A FEW YEARS AGO, I was listening to our resident evangelist preach about angels. During this sermon, he reminded us that we do indeed have a guardian angel assigned to us. What a warm and comforting thought! I have always appreciated the role the angel played in visiting Mary to announce the birth of Jesus. As he continued to preach, what came next was very disconcerting. He said, "You have a demon assigned to you as well." Hearing this was not creating feelings of warmth and hope. It was creating shock and fear. Although I intellectually knew the scriptures described the attacks of the enemy, I never realized I would be visited by a demon.

During one of my shifts at the hospital, as always, I was assigned four patients. One of them was in restraints, spoke no English, and had a one-on-one sitter. His family brought him to the emergency room because he became violent, started babbling, and would not eat or drink. When I assessed him, he was very agitated. He was hissing, spitting, kicking, and hitting. I spoke to the nurse tech in the room, told him to make sure the patient was safe and to protect himself. He looked very uncomfortable as he watched after this particular patient. I didn't blame him. I had a distinct feeling that something was very wrong here. Up to this point, this man led a normal life. He worked full time in the community and had a wife and children. All of his medical tests were normal. The doctors could not figure out what was wrong with him. Throughout the day, the behavior remained the same. There were no discernable words coming from him. It did not sound like any language I had ever heard. The nurse tech told me some family members came in and looked like they were performing some kind of ritual on him. At one point, I turned away from the patient to grab some gloves and the patient yelled "Sandra" in the most terrifying evil voice I had ever heard. I had never told him my name. How did he know what it was? There was terror in that room, and the nurse tech wanted out. Almost immediately, God reminded me that those who are saved are sealed in the Holy Spirit. The nurse tech was also a believer and a pastor's son. We comforted one another with the words of God and tried to recall every verse we had memorized, no matter what it was. We both knew that God would protect us and that we must depend on Him for strength and safety.

I don't know if you will ever encounter something like I did, but I was very glad I had prepared ahead of time by memorizing scripture and becoming familiar with doctrinal truth. Children of God cannot become demon-possessed. We cannot be "plucked out of the Father's hand" (John 10:28). I encourage you to start each day memorizing scripture. Write out one verse on a three-by-five card and take it with you wherever you go. Use a Bible app and listen to scripture throughout the day. Remember the truth of Ephesians 1:13–14. The whole book of Ephesians is a wonderful encouragement to all believers. Spend some time abiding with God and pray for one another. Have confidence, knowing that God will not leave your side.

Doctors were never able to figure out a rational medical reason or explanation for what happened to that patient. We fight a spiritual battle against a real enemy. Our defense is in our Savior, Jesus Christ. Start thinking about friends and relatives that don't know Him. Ask God to give you the strength to share the Gospel with them so that they can have the hope of eternity and the protection of the Holy Spirit. Be prepared to be salt and light wherever you go.

May God richly bless you as you dwell in His word. Every effort into memorizing scripture pays huge dividends for yourself and others. May you go forward in strength, grace, and confidence. God bless you.

When Someone Holds You Up in Prayer

DO YOU REMEMBER THE Bible story when the Israelites were in battle, and they prevailed against their enemy when Moses held his arms up? There are so many lessons that can be gleaned from this passage. Faith, obedience, and trust in God are just a few. Teamwork is another.

I have been a nurse for over thirty-seven years now. It's not an easy job. The challenges are many. The hours are long, and nurses are subjected to hours of suffering and pain with their patients and visiting family members. Doctors also typically yell and bark out orders, at times in a condescending manner. The phone rings constantly, and alarms go off throughout the entire day. Many times, I have thought of it as a battleground. Sickness is, after all, a result of the fallen world. We are far from that perfect Garden of Eden where Adam and Eve had fellowship with God. Dealing with sickness and suffering takes its toll on all nurses, both physically and emotionally. The day is spent juggling multiple critical issues all at once. In general, the twelve-hour shift is a string of chaotic moments intertwined with constant human suffering. Moment by moment, we make important decisions that have serious consequences. For some, it becomes too much, and they decide that it's not for them. Sometimes prayer is the only answer.

The reason I like this story about Moses is that it exposes a wonderful truth about God, friendship, and prayer. I have been lucky enough to have a fellow nurse who is my prayer partner. Some days, we work together, but most days we work opposite shifts. I feel this is where the magic begins. We have the unspoken understanding that we can text each other for prayer at any time during a shift. When the stress runs high and I'm overwhelmed, I text Kathleen and she prays. She knows what's going on, and what kind of a prayer is needed. Time and time again, prayers go up and relief comes. An aura of calm and order is felt as God's peace comes over the unit. That is God answering prayer. Just like Aaron and Hur held up Moses' arms, she holds me up in prayer. I do the same for her. It's the acting out of godly teamwork during times of battle and strife. It's beautiful and can be depended on.

Whose arms are you holding up? Find someone and become prayer partners. Devise a plan to help each other. Share the results and triumphs of each day. Battles are raging all around us, and we all need someone to hold us up. There is nothing like the feeling of supernatural peace and tranquility because someone is praying for you. This is one way we can show love to one another. Jesus Himself asked His friends to pray for Him. He was disappointed when they fell asleep. Enter into a partnership with a friend. Hold each other up in prayer. Create a relationship of trust and love. Become the friend that "sticks closer than a brother."

I pray that you will seek Him out to bless a friend in this way. You will be so glad you did. Encourage each other and share your triumphs in times of battle. He cares for you! He loves you! Gives thanks to Him by shouldering the burden of a friend. May God deeply bless you.

The Walls of Blackness Castle

RECENTLY, MY HUSBAND AND I visited Blackness Castle in Scotland. It is an impressive fortress completely made of stone. The walls are seventeen feet thick. The Scots meant business when they built it. Although their attempts at security were valiant, the walls were breached by Sir Oliver Cromwell in 1650.

Our modern homes have walls that are only inches thick. Generally, I feel pretty safe in my home. We make sure we lock the doors and set the alarm. I always look through the peephole when someone knocks. I trust the walls to be secure enough to protect me. My problem is more about fighting breaches that occur in my own mind. I am safe and secure behind the walls of my own home, but I have trouble shutting out the worries that plague my mind concerning work, family, or friends. I feel stressed when the accuser tries to make me feel like I'm not worthy of God's love and protection. If the accusations in me don't shut off, then even a seventeen-foot wall won't work.

This year, I have been learning about King David's struggle with his enemies. He had many. He saw death and destruction on all sides. One of the things that grieved him the most was his relationship with Saul. He was called to serve Saul, yet Saul became a very real threat to David's life. Saul tried to kill David on many occasions, but

David always respected the God-given authority given to Saul. David became known as "a man after God's own heart" because he displayed such transparency and boldness in his relationship with God.

Do you have struggles within the walls of your home? Do you have trouble relaxing after a busy day at work? Do problems rehearse themselves over and over in your mind? I believe that David figured out how to deal with these issues. He had a special relationship with God. His words are there to teach us that we can become "a woman after God's own heart."

First, David complained to God. Psalm 142:1–2 says, "I cried unto the LORD with my voice, with my voice unto the LORD did I make my supplication, I poured out my complaint before him, I showed before him my trouble." Sometimes I forget that God knows everything in my thoughts. He is waiting for me to acknowledge it back to Him. When you pour out your heart to Him, He will take the burden from you. Tell Him all your worries. Don't hold back. No matter how ugly it may be, He wants to hear it.

Next, read Romans chapter 8:31. Whenever I need a pep talk, this is where I go. "If God is for us, who can be against us." He promises us that nothing will separate us from His love. Do you ever lose confidence in your God-given role as a wife, mom, or professional? He sanctified you into that role, and He will in no way abandon you. He will enable you to carry out every detail of what He has called you to do. What comfort!

Lastly, be thankful. Replace negative thought patterns with songs of thanksgiving. Get out some paper and pencil and write down everything that comes to mind. There is nothing better than thankfulness to shock your brain out of a negative attitude! Read Psalm 100:4. If you are a parent, you know how wonderful it is when your child says, "Thank you." Our Heavenly Father loves to hear from us.

Although incredibly impressive, with seventeen-foot-thick walls, Blackness Castle was not able to keep the enemy at bay. We can stand firm, knowing that God provides protection for us on all sides, in all circumstances, and in all situations. His love and caring becomes an impenetrable spiritual castle with supernatural walls which protect us and cannot be breached!

Dear Heavenly Father,

I pray for any friends that are experiencing opposition in their lives at this moment. I pray that you will give them peace and strength. I pray that they will feel love and protection that only YOU can give.

I pray that they have the confidence to carry out the work that you have called them to do.

In Jesus's name, amen.

Epilogue

I HOPE YOU HAVE ENJOYED reading the words that came from my daily walks as much as I have enjoyed stepping out in faith to share these stories and lessons with you in this book. God never left me empty, and He continues to inspire me whenever I get outside to clear my head. Now it's your turn. You could choose ten Facebook, X (formerly Twitter), or Instagram friends and make a prayer group like I did. They will be so happy that someone is praying for them. Start by posting a Bible verse and tell them what it means to you. Use an attribute of God and give an example of how exploring the attribute gives hope and helps solve problems. Search for a mentor, and then see who you could be a mentor to. Find a prayer buddy and share how God is blessing you with answered prayer. Pick a subject like anxiety or fear and list all the verses that address these difficulties. Share what you are doing in your personal quiet time. Start a Wordgo group, a great app for individual and/or group Bible study. Get involved in discipleship programs at your church. There are endless ways to grow and encourage one another. Bible Study Fellowship is another great choice for exploring and learning about the Word of God and experiencing community. The Pocket Testament League will send you helpful booklets to help you share the Gospel. In this great nation of ours, we are so blessed with a variety of resources to enrich our walk with the Lord. I challenge you to seek out His will and step forward in confidence and hope. All of us are important to Him, and He wants to use us to enlarge His kingdom. Be a blessing to others. May you have His favor as you step forward for Him. God bless you, and again thank you for sharing my personal journey of faith and hope!

One Day I Dreamed

Taken from The Pilgrim Gospel Messenger

THIS LITTLE POEM WAS included in the back of my New Testament Bible. After reading it, I have never been the same. I pray you will read it, meditate on it, and contemplate your role in sharing the gospel message.

> One day as I was fast asleep
> I had this stirring dream
> I was caught up to be with God,
> With angels it did seem
> And while up there, I met Gods
> Saints, from many parts of earth,
> Now some were great and famous
> Men, and some of humble birth.
> I talked to one great saint of God
> The first one that I met
> He told me how he died for Christ,
> His words I can't forget
> He lived, he said in Bible days,

and died at Nero's stake
"It was a joy to give my all
And burn for Jesus' sake."
"I was so glad to die for Christ,"
With humble words he said,
And as I listened to it all
I bowed my guilty head.
Another man then gently spoke,
Here is my story, friend.
'Twas cannibals who took my life,
because I would not bend.
"I tried to tell those heathen souls
Of Christ who came to die.
They ate my flesh and drank my
Blood, but sent my soul on high
"Of course, up here are millions
More, with stories rare and true.
But friend, before I tell you more,
Let's hear your story too."
I was ashamed of how I'd failed,
I'd known no sacrifice.
I was ashamed of how I'd failed
I'd paid such little price.
I'd never given any funds
To send the gospel out.
I'd lived a life of luxury
And never done without.
Those costly cars, those extra clothes,
seem needless now and vain;
The very thought of how I'd lived,
Filled my heart with pain.
Just then it seemed that Jesus said,
Take up my cross today;
"I'll give you one more chance
To work and give and pray"
My guilty heart began to burn,

Boldly Encouraged

My nervous body shake
I then awoke with tear filled eyes
With new resolves to make.
I told the Lord from that day forth
My best, my all I'd give.
To win the lost in every place
For this alone I'd live.
I told the Lord that from then on
I would not waste a dime
That I would give myself to prayer
And really use my time.
That I would seek with all my heart
That power from above;
To help me tell a heathen world
Of Jesus' grace and love.

The Romans Road

AT SOME POINT IN time, a certain set of verses from the book of Romans became known as the Romans Road. There are most likely different variations, yet I will give you the four verses I use for my version. It is a good idea to memorize these verses. They are key in pointing out and delivering the gospel message.

The following verses constitute what is known as the Romans Road:

> For all have sinned and come short of the glory of God. (Romans 3:23)

> For the wages of sin is death: but the gift of God is eternal life through Jesus Christ our Lord. (Romans 6:23)

> But God commendeth His love towards us, in that, while we were yet sinners, Christ died for us. (Romans 5:8)

> For whosoever shall call upon the name of the Lord shall be saved. (Romans 10:13)

The Attributes of God

I HAVE FOUND THAT FOCUSING on the attributes of God is a very helpful tool, especially when you are facing difficulties. God has many attributes, and each one addresses different problems that we have. For example, God's mercy addresses the person in need of forgiveness. God's holiness reminds us that He is perfect and without fault. God's sovereignty reminds us that no matter what is going on, He is in complete control. I have a long list of His attributes and refer to them on a regular basis. I try to identify my problem and then use the list to retrieve the attribute that addresses that specific problem.

The Sinner's Prayer

THE SINNER'S PRAYER IS a guideline for helping a person take the step to receive Christ as their personal Savior. Remember that the Bible teaches us to "confess with your mouth and believe in your heart." This is not to be used as a vain repetition but as a heartfelt decision to turn away from sin and follow the Lord, depending on Him alone to provide eternal salvation.

> Dear God, I know that I am a sinner, and I ask for your forgiveness. I believe Jesus Christ is Your Son. I believe that He died for my sin and that You raised Him to life. I want to trust Him as my Savior and follow Him as Lord, from this day forward. Guide my life and help me to do Your will. I pray this in the name of Jesus. Amen.

Key Bible Verses for Special Situations

BIBLE VERSES HAVE BEEN so useful to me and have always strengthened me throughout my life and during life's challenging situations and trials. So I would highly encourage you all to develop your own arsenal of helpful verses and to keep them with you, so you have easy access to them for reference. Memorize a few favorites from verses that have helped you and keep them written on cards or on your mobile phone so that you can refer to them as needed. God may use you to encourage someone who is in need of help during a trial or a rough season in their life. It is so important to be ready and equipped at all times. Overall, what I have discovered is that as you seek His Word, hold his scriptures near you, and use these inspired words for yourself and others, God will bless you in so many ways during the process. It's a gift that truly keeps on giving!

Verses for anxiety: Psalm 94:19, Romans 8:38–39, Philippians 4:6–7

Verses for fear: 2 Timothy 1:7, Isaiah 35:4, Isaiah 41:10

Verses for depression: Deuteronomy 31:8, Philippians 4:8, Jeremiah 29:11

Verses for encouragement: John 16:33, Psalm 34:4–5, Psalm 94:18–19

Verses when you are looking for answers: Matthew 7:7, 2 Timothy 3:16, 1 Corinthians 10:13

Verses to fight evil. Ephesians 6:10–15, Isaiah 25:8, 2 Chronicles 31:1

About the Author

Sandra McManus is originally from Bellingham, Washington, and graduated from Seahome High School. She attended Rhode Island University and graduated with a bachelor of science degree (BSN) in nursing and has worked as a registered nurse (RN) for over thirty-seven years as a home care nurse and in various hospitals in Washington, Hawaii, and California. She has traveled the world with her husband Jeff, who was an Air Force officer and pilot and lived in Bangkok, Thailand, as part of their military diplomatic assignment with the American Embassy. She enjoys hiking, snorkeling, skiing, photography, and interactive adventures with wildlife. She is an avid knitter and delights in sharing her knowledge of nutrition with patients, family, and friends. She is a member of the Lancaster Baptist Church and also faithfully serves in Bible Study Fellowship (BSF) as a group leader. Sandra lives in Southern California with her husband, Jeff, and has two adult sons, Andrew and William, who reside in Texas and Thailand.